Michael Jai McKenzie is an American poet from Los Angeles, California. Although Michael was born in Los Angeles, he moved to Pasadena at the age of ten where he eventually attended Pasadena High School. McKenzie started writing short stories and poems at a very young age, and soon that desire to write lead him to publishing his first poetry book entitled *Thought Prints.*

To my wife, Diedra McKenzie, who inspired most of my poetry.

Michael Jai McKenzie

THOUGHT PRINTS

AUSTIN MACAULEY PUBLISHERS™
LONDON • CAMBRIDGE • NEW YORK • SHARJAH

Copyright © Michael Jai McKenzie 2024

All rights reserved. No part of this publication may be reproduced, distributed, or transmitted in any form or by any means, including photocopying, recording, or other electronic or mechanical methods, without the prior written permission of the publisher, except in the case of brief quotations embodied in critical reviews and certain other non-commercial uses permitted by copyright law. For permission requests, write to the publisher.

Any person who commits any unauthorized act in relation to this publication may be liable to criminal prosecution and civil claims for damages.

Ordering Information
Quantity sales: Special discounts are available on quantity purchases by corporations, associations, and others. For details, contact the publisher at the address below.

Publisher's Cataloging-in-Publication data
McKenzie, Michael Jai
Thought Prints

ISBN 9781685624361 (Paperback)
ISBN 9781685624378 (Hardback)
ISBN 9781685624392 (ePub e-book)
ISBN 9781685624385 (Audiobook)

Library of Congress Control Number: 2023910888

www.austinmacauley.com/us

First Published 2024
Austin Macauley Publishers LLC
40 Wall Street, 33rd Floor, Suite 3302
New York, NY 10005
USA

mail-usa@austinmacauley.com
+1 (646) 5125767

My mother and father for bringing me here, my aunties and uncles, my brother and my sister, for always having my back, no matter who didn't! Still do to this day! All parties in general who supported my journey!

All past, present, and future supporters who believe in me! I thank and acknowledge you for your motivation!

A Dream

I had a dream.
I was in a land surrounded by love and kindness. All in this land were patient and without judgement. There was a compassion between all there and joy seemed to seep into every human being around. There was love between one and another that only persisted to grow!
No hatred, No envy, No division, No enemies!
Just loving and giving…

As I continued to journey the paths of this beautiful place of peace and tranquility, I noticed a room in the distance. There was a mist that seemed to hover around the entrance of this un-explored room. My curiosity prevailed and I needed clarity about this room. I wondered why this was the only room with a presence not befitting the land. Why was this mist surrounding this door? Why was there a welcome sign? So I walked through all of the mist and entered the door.

As I entered, I was greeted with the sound of crying. There were streams of tears crashing against both sides of the walkway. The people seemed lost and loveless. This place was without compassion or love. There were no groups of people, only individuals. There was no laughter or joy, just eerie chuckles. No one was helping one another. Every person here was serving themselves even at the expense of another. Every person here was committed to serving only there wants and desires. The infliction of pain and selfishness was all around this place.

I noticed a very old man standing in the corner of this room who appeared to possess a certain wisdom about this place. Unlike the others, he had a troubled look on his face as if he didn't approve of this place. I walked over to him and asked "What of this place? Why are there so many hurting souls and broken spirits? Why is it so dark in here? Why is this place riddled with pain and anguish beyond any I've known? Where are we?"

The wise man looked around this cold dark room filled with turmoil and corruption and sadly replied

"We're awake!"

A Letter to Myself...

Birthed in a month on a day, somewhere in time, somewhere in history, somewhere in my past I didn't exist...but I was to be.
When I look back in time exploring my mind, I realize I didn't glance...
But I was to see...
I should've explored deeper into things I couldn't conceive.
But I was locked inside a padded cell called me, unable to perceive.
Birthed in a month on a day, somewhere in time.
Somewhere in history.
Confusing myself as if life had no mystery...once stuck on lost thoughts wishfully...
Searching for dignity...but in reality I was en-crippling me...
Who actually defines prosperity?
Is it I or he who defies me?
Birthed in a month on a day, somewhere in time.
Somewhere in history.
Who or what determines victory...was I born inside an empty being?
And I did confide in empty things...

Believing it true when it was deceiving.
The plot is misleading…
I see there's no book yet, I still think I'm reading.
Birthed in a month on a day, somewhere in time.
Somewhere in history.
I called it a nitch…
But I let life cause much strife and my gift didn't lift.
Then I looked at a ditch…
The lessons I learned from all of the turns that I carelessly missed.
One day I was filled with pride…
Then I studied the mirror and the reflection didn't lie.
Still I couldn't figure out why…
Are the answers I seek somewhere deep inside?
Is there still time left?
Should I hurt only internally and never confess?
All the times I chased wealth…
Then connected with women who didn't wish me the best….
How can two make one less?
How could I be naked when I never undressed?
I think it's time to self-reflect…
For now indeed, I must now proceed…
And write a letter to myself…

Again

A MEETING IN SPRING, LEAD US TO THIS THING
THAT HAS BLOSSOMED INTO A ROSE
A FLOWER HAS GROWN, AND ALL ON ITS OWN
AS ALL OF LOVE'S PEDALS UNFOLD
YOU'VE TAKEN MY HAND, ON OUR LOVE WE STAND
FOR LIFE WE HAVE TAKEN A VOW
I'VE FOUND MY NEW TREASURE, IT'S US NOW FOREVER
WITH NO LOVE DISTURBANCE ALLOWED
SOME DAYS I THINK BACK, ONE HISTORICAL FACT
OUR LOVE HAS SURVIVED MANY TESTS
BUT THE TESTS ONLY LACK, IF TRUE LOVE IS IN TACT
NO NEGATIVE HEARTS MANIFEST
I'VE RESEARCHED THIS WORLD, I'VE STUDIED ALL PEARLS
BUT YOU ARE BEYOND DEFINITION
I'VE SEEN WEATHER CHANGE, BUT YOU STAY THE SAME

YOU LOVE ME WITH SO MUCH CONVICTION
WHEN YOU'RE NEXT TO ME, IT FEELS MAKE BELIEVE
LIKE I WILL AWAKE FROM MY SLEEP
YOUR LOVE IS MY GUIDE, WITH YOU AS MY BRIDE
I KNOW THAT MY LIFE WILL SUCCEED
LOVE'S SHOWN ME THE TRUTH, ALL ALONG IT WAS YOU
TRUE LOVE STARTING OUT AS TRUE FRIENDS
NOW DAY AFTER DAY, I WAKE TO YOUR FACE
FALLING IN LOVE ALL OVER AGAIN

Am I...

AM I THE PRODUCT OF WHAT SOCIETY SAYS I AM?
OR AM I WHO THEY THINK I SHOULD BE?
AM I A MALE BECAUSE SOCIETY SAYS I'M A MAN?
OR AM I WHAT THEY'VE DECIDED IS HE?
AM I LOST BECAUSE SOCIETY SAYS I'M FOUND?
OR AM I MAKING NOISE WITHOUT SOUND?
AM I HIGH BECAUSE SOCIETY SAYS I CAN FLY?
OR AM I ONLY FLYING IN MY MIND?
AM I A KING BECAUSE SOCIETY SEES THERE'S A CROWN?
OR AM I REALLY JUST SOCIETY'S CLOWN?
AM I A HAWK BECAUSE SOCIETY SAYS I HAVE WINGS?
OR CAN I ONLY TAKE FLIGHT IN MY DREAMS?
IS THERE A TEAR IN MY FACE BECAUSE THEY SAY I CAN WEEP?
OR DO THE TEARS IN MY EYES MAKE ME WEAK?

AM I STRONG TO MY CORE BECAUSE THEY SAY I HAVE STRENGTH?
OR AM I LOST BECAUSE THEY SAY I CAN'T WIN?
AM I A FORCE BECAUSE SOCIETY GAVE ME THE CHOICE?
OR DO THEY SILENCE THE SOUND OF MY VOICE?
AM I A STRONG SOLID WIND BECAUSE THEY GAVE ME THE AIR?
OR DO THEY LOOK AT ME AND BLINDLY STARE?
AM I A THOUGHT IN MY MIND BECAUSE THEY TELL ME TO THINK?
OR DO I USE MY OWN BRAIN TO SUCCEED?
AM I THE ONE WHO WILL RISE ABOVE ALL THE LINES?
OR DO I BELIEVE THAT THE GROUND IS MY SKY?
AM I A SOUL OF MY OWN WHO WILL CONQUER IT ALL?
OR WILL I ALLOW SOCIETY'S PLAN FOR MY FALL?
AM I WALKING THROUGH LIFE IN SOCIETY'S SHOES?
OR ARE MY FEET WALKING IN TRUTH?
ARE THEY HEARING THE MUSIC 'CAUSE THEY GAVE ME A SONG?
OR ARE THE LYRICS THEY'RE HEARING ALL WRONG?

AM I SHINING INSIDE 'CAUSE THEY GAVE ME THE SUN?
OR HAS ONLY THE STORM JUST BEGUN?
HAVE THEY GIVEN ME SMILES 'CAUSE THEY SAID I COULD LAUGH?
OR AM I DESIGNED TO BE SAD?
AM I LOCKED DEEP INSIDE ALL THEIR REALMS OF CONFUSION?
OR DO I RECOGNIZE THEIR ILLUSION?
AM I LOST DEEP INSIDE THE ABUSE OF A LOVER
'CAUSE THEY ONLY LOVE ME UNDERCOVER?
AM I FALLING DOWN ONLY IGNITING THEIR RISE?
FORE IT'S REALLY MY CLIMB THEY DESPISE
AM I ONLY TO LIVE 'CAUSE THEY SAY I EXIST
OR AM I SIMPLY PART OF A LIST?
AM I ONLY TO LEARN WHAT THEY WANT ME TO KNOW?
TO DISRUPT THE TRUE PATH OF MY SOUL

AM I JUST A CREATION OF WHAT I'M SUPPOSED TO BE?
AM I SOCIETY'S VERSION OF ME...?

AM I...?

Armor

THE BATTLES BEGUN THE SOLDIERS SET
DESIGNED TO DIVIDE EVERY CLICK
THEY DON'T ONLY FIGHT THE WAR OF THE BLESSED
THEY FIGHT 'TIL THEY KILL EVERY KISS
THE BOMBS THEY DEPLOY EXPLODE OUR LOVE
BUT ONLY IF WE LET THEM IN
THE CALM BEFORE STORM
THAT SUBTLE TOUCH
THAT THING THAT TAKES US TO THE END
THEY FIGHT TO DIVIDE EVERY CONNECT
IF WE SHOW LOVE BEYOND DIVISION
THEY WILL UNDERMINE WITH NO RESPECT
FINDING JOY IN OUR LOVES COLLISION
THE WICKED IN HEART WILL NEVER STOP
THEY WILL USE ALL BOMBS TO DESTROY
WE CANNOT LET BOMBERS MAKE US DROP
THIS BATTLE OUR HEARTS MUST ENDURE
THEY SHOOT MISSILES HIGH TO BREAK OUR CORE
WE MUST BE ABOVE ALL THEIR ROCKETS
THEIR FIRING HIGH TO MAKE US SORE

LOVE MUST OUTWEIGH ATTEMPTS TO BLOCK IT
THE CAPTAINS LEAD THEM TO COME BETWEEN
WHAT WE HAVE BUILT BEYOND CONCEPTION
THIS WAR WE CAN WIN OUR LOVE IS DEEP
OUR LOVE CAN RISE ABOVE DECEPTION
THE BATTLE GROUNDS COLD THE TANKS ARE THERE
BUT WE'RE READY FOR THE ATTACK
THEY WON'T FIND THE MOLD TO KILL OUR CARE
OUR LOVE'S SENDING MORE MISSILES BACK
WE'VE BEATEN THEIR STRIKES TO SLOW US DOWN
EFFORTS TO CAUSE MISERABLE PAIN
THE SOLDIERS CANNOT CREATE A FROWN
OUR LOVE STILL OWNS A SMILING FACE
THEY TRY TO KILL HOPE THAT WE'LL STAY ALIVE
THEY TRY TO SHOOT THEIR MISSILES FARTHER
AND FINALLY WE SHOW THAT WE CAN SURVIVE
BEHIND OUR TRUE LOVE'S COAT OF ARMOR

Champagne

THE CELEBRATION BEGINS FOR OUR LIFELONG LOVE
A CELEBRATION OF FRIENDS THAT HAVE BECOME ONE
THE ELEVATION IS HERE AND FOR LIFE WE'RE UNITED
NO HESITATION OR FEAR FOR OUR HEARTS HAVE DECIDED
NO MORE GLOOM IN OUR LIFE, WE HAVE FOUND UNREAL
NO MORE DOOM IN OUR NIGHT'S CLOSENESS CAN'T UNSEAL
ANOTHER CHEERFUL DAY TO FACE THANKS TO ALL YOU ARE
ALL OTHER TEARFUL DAYS ERASED, YOU'VE UNDONE MY SCARS
I NEVER KNEW YOUR LOVELINESS WOULD BE MY GIFT
I'LL NEVER LOSE YOUR LOVING KISS AND MY LIFE RISK
A CELEBRATION IS NEAR TO UPLIFT OUR LIFE

A DEDICATION TOWARDS YEARS THAT WE'VE SHARED ON HIGH
I AM GRATEFUL FOR YOU AND MY HEART IS REMINDED
EVERYDAY OF YOUR LOVE AND THE TRUST YOU'VE INVITED
A DESTRUCTIVE WORLD BUT YOU MINIMIZE DISASTER
MY SEDUCTIVE PEARL, YOU HAVE BECOME MY MASTER
INCOMPLETE WAS I, BEFORE YOUR LOVE LIGHT CAME
IN TOO DEEP IS MY MIND, YOUR LOVE STRUCK UNTAMED
A CELEBRATION OF US AND THE LIFE WE'VE GAINED
YOU AND I, ALL OUR LOVE, AND A GLASS OF CHAMPAGNE

Closed

I CAME ACROSS AN OPEN DOOR, IT CREAKED
BUT WHAT DID I ACTUALLY FIND
DISTRACTED BY THE SOCIAL SORE, WE SEEK
IN TRUTH, WE ARE ACTUALLY BLIND

I CAME ACROSS A HEARTFELT LOVE, I THOUGHT
BUT IT ONLY LIVED IN MY HEAD
DISTRACTED BY A PLASTIC HUG, I LOST
I LAID IN A PERILOUS BED

I CAME ACROSS A PATH OF LIES, NO TRUTH
A ROAD OF TRUE DECEPTION
DISTRACTED BY THE PLASTIC WISE, NO VIEW
ALL ACTING OUT CONNECTION

I CAME ACROSS A LIGHTED LANE, THE BRIGHTEST
BUT SOON THE LANE GOT DARK
DISTRACTED AS THE LIGHTING FADES, NOW LIGHTLESS
SOME PAINTINGS AREN'T TRUE ART

I CAME ACROSS A SOLID ROCK, IT CRUMBLED
THE MOMENT I SAW STONE
DISTRACTED BY A KEYLESS LOCK, I STRUGGLED
LOCKED IN THE DANGER ZONE

I CAME ACROSS THE COLDEST HEARTS, JUST ICY
PRETENDING TO BE WARM
DISTRACTED BY THEIR PHONY PARTS, JUST FRIGHTENING
ALLURING WITH FALSE CHARM

I CAME ACROSS A FLYING BIRD, BUT WINGLESS
PRETENDING TO TAKE FLIGHT
DISTRACTED BY THEIR LYING WORDS, BUT SEE LESS
JUST GAZING WITHOUT SIGHT

I CAME ACROSS A BEAUTY QUEEN, BUT CROWNLESS
A SELF PROCLAIMED PRINCESS
DISTRACTED BY DILUTED SCHEMES, COUNTLESS
DECEPTION ALL SEEMED ENDLESS

I CAME ACROSS A PHOTOGRAPH, NO IMAGE
A FACELESS, SMILELESS, STILL
DISTRACTED BY THE FADED MASK, NO FEELING
JUST HEARTLESS VEINS OF CHILL

I CAME ACROSS AN OPEN DOOR, I ENTERED AND FOUND A DARKER ROAD
CONVINCED IT WAS AN OPEN DOOR, WHEN REALLY
THE DOOR WAS ACTUALLY CLOSED

Crowded

That tender touch, that perfect kiss
How your voice sings to me
That gentle love, that perfect wish
You've granted perfectly
That warm embrace, the way you hold
How you caress my mind
That lovely face, my centerfold
My vintage glass of wine
That mental stroke, internal bliss
You are my inner smile
A simple note, eternalness
You are my life, worthwhile
That subtle purr, that soothing laugh
Confirming happiness
The way you yearn, for all I am
Without you I am less
Your passion burns, inside my soul
My heart now filled with flames
You've captured nerves, you taken hold
And rendered me insane
Your lovely scent, your dreamy touch
You hypnotize my thoughts

You've shattered myths, about true love
Belief no longer lost
You've made it real, that love inside
That thing I've always doubted
My brain is filled, of your love high
Of you, my thoughts are crowded

Distortion

WHEN WILL WE ACCEPT THAT STRIFE AND STRESS
CAN TAKE ON SO MANY FORMS
WHY DO WE REJECT WHAT WOULD BE THE BEST
INVITING AN UN-NEEDED STORM

WHEN WILL WE REALIZE, OUR TRUE PURPOSE LIES
IN HOW WE CAN SEE OURSELVES
BUT LOST IN OUR MINDS AS IF BY DESIGN
BECAUSE WE CAN'T RECOGNIZE WEALTH

WHEN WILL WE BELIEVE THE WORDS LIFE SPEAKS
WHENEVER THEY'RE SHOUTED SO LOUD
WE JUST CLOSE OUR EARS TO ALL THAT WE HEAR
THEN SOON WE GET USED BY THE CROWD

WHEN CAN WE UNDO OUR LIFE'S SET OF RULES
DICTATING HOW EVERY MIND WORKS

HOW COME WE DON'T USE OUR POWER TO MOVE
ON GROUND WHERE WE CONQUER OUR HURT

WHEN CAN WE RELAX AND BASE LIFE ON FACTS
AND NOT ON THE VIEW OF OUR PEERS
FOR WHEN WE LOOK BACK ON OUR LIFE'S COLLAPSE
WE SEE ALL OUR PAIN MADE THEM CHEER

WHEN DO WE ADMIT THAT WE ARE EQUIPPED
TO USE OUR OWN BRAIN TO DECIDE
WE WON'T SEE OUR GIFT BEYOND ALL THE MIST
UNLESS WE CLEAR SMOKE FROM OUR EYES

WHEN DO WE UNTIE THE KNOTS IN OUR MINDS
THAT KEEP US IN BONDAGE, CALLED US
A LOCK IN OUR HEAD THAT HURTS US INSTEAD
AND KEEPS US BEHIND IN OUR THRUST

WHEN WILL WE HAVE SIGHT FOR ALL OF OUR LIFE
AND VIEW IT IN ITS TRUE PROPORTION
WILL WE EVER FIND THE ROOT OF LIFE'S LIES
SURVIVING BEHIND THE DISTORTION

Divided

CONNECTED AS ONE, THE MOMENT WE MET
A UNION FOR ALL FUTURE GAZERS
WE'VE NOW TAKEN FLIGHT, AS IF IN A JET
AND OUR LOVE IS FLIGHT'S ELEVATOR
WE WERE MADE TO SOAR, ABOVE ALL THE WEATHER
AND NOW WE JUST GLIDE THROUGH THE AIR
WE CAN'T SEE THE FLOOR,
OUR HIGHS JUST WON'T LET US
IT'S AS IF THE FLOOR ISN'T THERE
OUR WINGS NOW EXPAND, TO MAKE US FLY HIGHER
OUR LOVE LIFTS US BEYOND THE SKY
OUR DEEPNESS COMMANDS, WE'LL NEVER EXPIRE
OUR LOVE WILL SURVIVE BEYOND LIFE
WE USED TO BE TWO, BEFORE WE INVESTED
IN OUR HEART'S TRUE LOVE TAKING SHAPE
AND NOW WE ARE GLUE, OUR LOVE IS A TREASURE
FOREVER STILL GUIDING OUR WAY

YOU'VE ENTERED MY SOUL, MY MIND AND MY SPIRIT
AND NOW YOU ARE HOW I SURVIVE
YOU'VE TAKEN CONTROL, AND I USED TO FEAR IT
AND NOW YOUR LOVE KEEPS ME ALIVE
YOU ARE BUT A PEARL, IN A SEA FULL OF DIAMONDS
BUT YOU SHINE BEYOND EVERY JEWEL
OUR LOVE HAS UNFURLED, ITS NO LONGER HIDING
THERE'S NO REGULATIONS OR RULES
WE NOW SHARE A BOND, A CLOSENESS AND DEPTH
OUR LOVE CAN BE SEEN BY UNSIGHTED
OUR LOVE IS SO STRONG, A DEPTH NEVER FELT
FOR LIFE OUR LOVE CAN'T BE DIVIDED

Enough

I'VE FOUND A WAY TO COPE WITH STRAIN
WHEN YOU'RE NOT IN MY ARMS
I LOVE YOU SO, I MISS YOUR HOLD
YOUR ABSENCE BRINGS ME HARM
I'VE CALLED YOUR NAME A THOUSAND WAYS
JUST KNOWING YOU WILL HEAR
IT'S EVERY WORD YOU'VE EVER HEARD
AS OUR LOVE PERSEVERES
I'M SIMPLY WEAK FROM ALL YOUR SWEET
EMPOWERED BY YOUR SOUL
YOU'RE ALL I SEEK AND ALL I NEED
UNTIL WE BOTH GROW OLD
I HAVE THE TASK OF ALL ROMANCE
CONNECTING OUR HEART STRINGS
TO SERVE MY QUEEN, MAKE TRUE YOUR
DREAMS
BEYOND ALL FANTASIES
I OFTEN WISH I COULD MAKE SENSE
OF HOW DEEP THINGS COULD GET
HOW OFTEN IS A LOVE LIKE THIS
A MIND-BLOWING EVENT
I HAVE BEEN ASKED TIMES IN THE PAST

JUST HOW DEEP IS MY LOVE
THERE IS NO END, NO MEASURED MASS
IT'S NEVER DEEP ENOUGH

Fiction

AT TIMES OUR LOVE SEEMS SO UNREAL
I CAN'T BELIEVE IT'S TRUE
AND HOW YOU GLOW WITH SUCH APPEAL
I CAN'T BELIEVE IT'S YOU
AT TIMES I FIND I DOUBT MYSELF
YOUR RADIANCE IS SO
YOU'VE MADE ME RICH WITH YOUR LOVE'S WEALTH
I CAN'T BELIEVE YOU'RE GOLD
I FEEL SO RICH BECAUSE OF US
I'VE WON THE LOTTERY
I FEEL NO DITCH CAN STUMBLE WHAT
WE'VE UNITED SOLIDLY
AT TIMES I LOOK INTO YOUR EYES
AND SEE YOUR TEARS OF JOY
SOMETIMES I FEEL A KID INSIDE
AND YOUR LOVE IS MY TOY
I HOLD YOU CLOSE, CLENCHING SO TIGHT
WHEN YOU ARE IN MY ARMS
I CAN'T BELIEVE IT FEELS SO RIGHT
NO FLAGS AND NO ALARMS
AT TIMES I SEE YOUR LOVELY FACE

AND FALL DOWN ON THE ROAD
YOU MAKE ME RUN WHEN THERE'S NO RACE
I SCORE WITHOUT A GOAL
SOMETIMES I'M LOST INSIDE A MAZE
BUT I FIND US WITH EASE
SOMETIMES I'M LOST INSIDE A DAZE
BUT YOU'RE IN DAZE WITH ME
I'VE SEARCHED SO LONG FOR YOU, MY GIFT
BUT ONLY TO FIND LIES
I NEVER THOUGHT I'D EVER GET
THE LOVE OF MY LIFETIME
AT TIMES I FIND I CAN'T BELIEVE
OUR LOVE'S FULL OF SUCH CONVICTION
IT'S JUST SO DEEP, MADE PERFECTLY
SO GOOD IT FEELS JUST LIKE FICTION

Growl...

You are the model of defiance
Defying all laws of existence
Your beauty has tilted compliance
It's lived only in my wishes

You have become the breath of me
The air that keeps me here
I now realize my destiny
Is tied to you, my dear

You'll never have a simple clue
Of how in love I am
It's all about the simple you
That makes me such a man

You captured me the day we met
And we were on our way
To falling deep and endlessly
In love till end of days

You've taught me that I can believe
In fantasies that walk

You're every dream I couldn't conceive
You're language when I talk

Fulfilling all my needs beyond
You are beyond belief
Whenever I feel life could go wrong
Your love brings me relief

You are the model of my sleep
So am I now awake
You've blinded all I thought I'd seen
With just your lovely face

You show me how you love me so
Without even one try
It naturally shows what's in your soul
It's something you can't hide

You are forever deep inside
And you should take a bow
Since you've become my lovely bride
You've made my heartbeat growl

If I...

IF I TELL YOU, I LOVE YOU WITH ALL OF MY HEART...
WILL YOU HATE ME WITH ALL OF YOURS?
IF I HOPE THAT OUR LOVE WILL NEVER DEPART...
WILL YOU SUDDENLY CLOSE YOUR HEART'S DOOR?
IF I SHOW YOU MY LOVE WILL SURVIVE TILL THE END...
WILL YOU SHOW ME WE WILL NEVER LAST?
IF I SEE THAT YOU ARE MY LOVER AND FRIEND...
WILL YOU SHOW ME THAT IT'S JUST A MASK?
IF I CHERISH OUR LOVE AND DEEPLY BELIEVE...
WILL YOU SHOW ME I CANNOT TRUST?
IF I SHOW YOU MY LOVE HAS THE STRONGEST WINGS...
WILL YOU SAY I CAN'T FLY HIGH ENOUGH?
IF I HOLD YOU SO TIGHT THAT WE BECOME ONE...
WILL YOU SAY THAT YOU DON'T NEED MY TOUCH?

IF I TOLD YOU WE MET AND THEN MY LIFE BEGUN…
WILL YOU SHOW ME I DON'T MEAN THAT MUCH?
IF I TELL YOU I ONLY HAVE EYES JUST FOR YOU…
WILL YOU SHOW ME THAT MY EYES ARE BLIND?
IF I TELL YOU YOUR ABSENCE WOULD MAKE ME SO BLUE…
WOULD YOU TELL ME YOU WERE NEVER MINE?
IF I GLOW EVERY MOMENT YOU WALK IN A ROOM…
WOULD YOU SHOW ME THAT YOUR GLOW IS DIM?
IF I SAY THAT I HAVE THE HEART OF A FOOL…
WOULD YOU SHOW ME THAT I'M TRULY HIM?

IF I SHOW YOU MY LOVE WILL ALWAYS REMAIN…
WILL YOU SHOW ME A LIFE FULL OF PAIN?
IF I TELL YOU OUR LOVE HAS IMPACTED MY BRAIN…
WOULD YOU SHOW ME THAT I AM INSANE?

IF I…

Impaired

I AM NOW COMPLETE BECAUSE I'VE BEEN MADE WHOLE
YOU HAVE ENTERED ME SO DEEP DOWN IN MY SOUL
I AM NOW A MAN WITH STRENGTH OF TWENTY MULES
AND IT'S ALL BECAUSE OF POWER, I CALL YOU
I AM NOW A FLOATER LIVING IN THE SKY
FOR YOU ARE THE LIFT THAT MAKES ME FLOAT SO HIGH
I AM NOW MORE THAN I'VE EVER BEEN BEFORE
IT'S THE LOVE YOU GIVE THAT'S TURNED ME INTO MORE
I AM NOW A MAN THAT HUNGERS EVERY DAY
FOR THAT TENDER LOVE THAT YOU PLACE UPON MY PLATE
I AM NOW A BEE BUZZING FOR YOUR POLLEN
AND I CAN'T BELIEVE THAT FLOWER I HAVE GOTTEN
I AM NOW A POET WRITING DEEPER LYRICS

YOU HAVE GIVEN ME A GLOW INSIDE MY SPIRIT
I AM NOW THE SILENT SCREAMER WHEN YOU'RE AROUND
FOR YOUR BEAUTY TAKES THE PLACE OF ALL THE SOUND
I AM NOW SO BRAVE, THOUGH ONCE MY HEART WAS SCARED
AND WITHOUT YOUR LOVE, MY HEART WOULD BE IMPAIRED

Life...

Although you wake to me every morning, throughout the day you remain sleep
Although you seek out much power and strength, you consistently remain weak

Although you thrive for me to be better, you only make me worse
Although you subscribe to my happy letter, you write a miserable verse

Although you buy into the ideal of dream me, only the nightmare lives
Although you shout you silently scream me, from the nightmare within

Although you open your eyes to blindness, you faithfully focus on sight
Although the clarity's there for the wisest, the cloudiness governs your mind

Although you seek the calm for your soul, you only find sounds of your yell

Although you seek courage to be bold, your fear keeps you locked in your hell

Although you think you're living real, you only reside in your plastic
Although you stay lost in your will, your outlook on me will be tragic

Although there are doors to be opened, your path leads to only the locked
Although you promote what is hopeless, it turns all your cans to cannots

Although you reside in a mansion, your mind keeps you locked in a shack
Although in your mind you are handsome, your mind is the beauty you lack

Although you feel you're together, you're actually falling apart
Although you think you are great weather, it's cold in your thunderous heart

Although you believe in your methods, you're building a bottomless pit
Although you believe you're not headless, your vision keeps you in the mist

Although you feel you are respected, you are only mocked in the dark

Although you make others rejected, you're painting a picture-less art

Although you feel you've solved the puzzle, you still have just not seen the light
Your physical being will only struggle, until your mind can reside in real life

Make Believe

I MET YOU THE DAY, THE LIE SHOWED ITS FACE
PARADING AROUND AS THE TRUTH
AS YOU DID PORTRAY, WHAT SEEMED WAS YOUR GRACE
WAS REALLY A MUSIC-LESS FLUTE
MY HEART MET DEMISE, ONE LOOK IN YOUR EYES
THAT SEEMED TO BE PUPILS OF LOVE
MY HEART MET SURPRISE, AS YOUR HEART DEVISED
TO PRETEND IT CAME FROM ABOVE
MY SOUL WAS DEFILED, BY YOUR SUBTLE SMILE
DESIGNED TO ENTICE MY BELIEF
THAT YOU WERE SINCERE, BUT TRUTH BECAME CLEAR
YOUR MOTIVE REVEALED ALL DECEIT
MY HEAD WAS CONFUSED, AS YOU SEEMED AMUSED
TO INFLICT ALL PAIN TO MY LIFE

MY TRUST NOW ABUSED, WHAT ONCE WAS MY MUSE
HAS TURNED OUT TO BE JUST A KNIFE
MY FOCUS IS DAZED, FROM ALL OF THE DAYS
I'VE SPENT THINKING YOU WERE MY SUN
YOUR MOTIVE REMAINS, TO BRING ME THE RAIN
AS FOR THE SUNSHINE THERE WAS NONE
I'VE REFRESHED MY MIND, AND LEFT LIES BEHIND
I COULD NOT SEE WHAT FATE CONCEIVED
THAT LOOK IN YOUR EYES, WAS MERELY A SIGN
THAT SADLY YOU WERE MAKE BELIEVE

My Oh My

MY OH MY
I CAN'T FATHOM BEAUTY AT THE LEVEL YOU DISPLAY

TRY MY EYES
I CAN SEE YOU IN VISIONS AS I DREAM OF YOUR FACE

MY OH MY
I CAN'T COMPREHEND HOW WE'VE BECOME SO CLOSE

WISE MY MIND
OUR LOVE'S SO INTENSE THAT I CAN'T HELP BUT BOAST

MY OH MY
MY HEART IS NOW YOURS UNTIL LIFE IS NO MORE

CRY OH CRY
YOUR TEARS FULL OF JOY THAT CONTINUE TO POUR

MY OH MY
THE PASSION BETWEEN US RECHARGES OUR HEARTS

TRY OH TRY
TO MENTALLY HANDLE THE TIMES WE'RE APART

MY OH MY
YOU BRING ME A JOY BEYOND ANY I'VE KNOWN

BYE OH BYE
TO ALL FUTURE PAINS AND THE PAST ONES I HOLD

MY OH MY
A BREATH OF FRESH AIR IS OUR LOVE IN MY LIFE

SIGH OH SIGH
WHENEVER I HOLD YOU EMBRACING YOU TIGHT

MY OH MY
THE HIGHER YOU TAKE ME THE HIGHER I GO

FLY OH FLY
YOU KEEP ME IN SPACE WITH THE LOVE THAT YOU OWN

MY OH MY
YOU STILL MAKE ME SHIVER WHEN I'M KISSIN' YOU

SHY OH SHY
YOU STILL MAKE ME QUIVER LIKE A NERVOUS FOOL

MY OH MY
AND NOW WE ARE BOUND BY THE LOVE THAT'S BECOME

TIE OH TIE
THE KNOT THAT NOW BINDS US CANNOT BE UNDONE

MY OH MY
AND THERE IS NO QUESTION ABOUT OUR CONNECT

WHY OH WHY
WOULD I EVER QUESTION THE LOVE YOU POSSESS

MY OH MY
WE RIDE ON FOREVER IN LOVE'S HORSE AND CARRIAGE

TIME OH TIME
EVEN WHEN LIFE'S ENDED OUR LOVE WILL NOT PERISH

MY OH MY OH MY…

My Peasant Clothes

LOVE IS NOT ABOUT A BANK DEPOSIT GOING THROUGH
IT'S WHEN I'M DOWN AND OUT, BUT STILL ON TOP TO YOU
I CAN DO A SHOW AND SING ALL THE RIGHT CHORDS
BUT LOVE IS WHEN I'M OFF KEY, BUT STILL YOU SING ALONG
IT'S NOT ABOUT A CONTEST THAT I WON
IT'S WHEN THEY BOO ME OFF THE STAGE, AND I STILL GET YOUR APPLAUSE
LOVE IS NOT ABOUT ME FLYING VERY HIGH
IT'S WHEN I'M ON THE GROUND, BUT YOU SEE ME IN THE SKY
IT'S NOT A TRIP TO A PARADISE ESCAPADE
LOVE IS WHEN RIGHT AT HOME IS A ROMANTIC GET AWAY
IT'S NOT ABOUT ME GIVING YOU THE STARS AND GALAXY
IT'S WHEN YOU FLOAT AROUND BECAUSE OF ME, DEFYING GRAVITY

IT IS NOT HOW MUCH I DAZZLE YOU WITH
DIAMONDS
IT'S WHEN WE'RE IN A CROWD, BUT IT'S JUST US
ON AN ISLAND
LOVE DOES NOT FADE AWAY WITH TIME
IT'S WHEN THE CLOCK IS NON-EXISTENT
BECAUSE OF WHAT WE FEEL INSIDE
IT IS NOT ABOUT A THRILL THAT I COULD GIVE
YOU EVERYDAY
LOVE IS ALL ABOUT THE THRILL YOU FEEL, JUST
WHEN YOU SEE MY FACE
IT IS NOT ABOUT A TREASURE CHEST YOU GIVE
ME, FULL OF JEWELS
IT'S WHEN I'M PENNILESS BUT RICH BECAUSE OF
YOU

LOVE IS NOT ABOUT A ROBE AND GOWN WE
WEAR FROM HEAD TO TOE

IT IS NOT ABOUT US WALKING AROUND ON
STREETS ALL PAVED IN GOLD

IT IS NOT ABOUT THE CROWNS WE WEAR TO
MAKE US SHINE AND GLOW

IT'S WHEN YOU'RE A QUEEN TO ME…

AND ONLY A KING YOU SEE…

EVEN IN MY PEASANT CLOTHES

Never Met

AND THAT DAY HAS PASSED THAT WE HAVE CROSSED PATHS
SINCE THAT DAY WE HAVE NOT LOOKED BACK
FOR THAT DAY DID LAST AND OUR AFTERMATH
HAS TURNED OUR HEART'S LOVE INTO FACT
AND ONCE IN OUR MINDS, WE WOULD NEVER FIND
THAT LOVE THAT'S BEEN LOST, OH SO LONG
DEFYING ALL TIME LOVE LIFTED SO HIGH
LOVE'S MUSIC'S ETERNITY'S SONG
AND ONCE IN OUR SOUL WE'D NEVER GROW OLD
WITHOUT OUR HEARTS LIFE LASTING BOND
WE NOW HAVE A HOLD OF EACH OTHER'S SOUL
OUR LOVE HAS US FLOATING BEYOND
AND ONCE IN OUR EYES WE SAW LOVES DEMISE
AND CLARITY WAS SO FAR AWAY
AND TO OUR SURPRISE AN INFINITE RISE

OUR BOND SAYING WORDS WE CAN'T SAY
AND ONCE IN THAT TOUCH, WE WANTED SO MUCH
BUT ONCE BELIEVED WE WOULD NOT FEEL
MY ROCKET SOARS UP, YOUR LOVE IS MY THRUST
AND LOVE HAS BROUGHT FORTH THE UNREAL
AND ONCE IN A DREAM THIS FANTASY SEEMED
TO LIVE ONLY IN OUR SLEEP
NOW LOVE HAS REDEEMED TO US WE DID CLEAVE
INTO AN UNMEASURABLE DEEP
AND NOW WE'RE SO CLOSE, OUR LOVE IS THE HOST
IT'S AS IF WE ARE THE PERFECT SET
OUR LOVE IS SO TRUE, IT'S NEVER BEEN NEW
IT'S LIKE OUR TWO HEARTS NEVER MET

No Cure

I'M FULLY INFECTED, BY OUR LOVE'S CONNECTION
BEFORE I WAS ILL WITHOUT YOU
I'M FULLY PROTECTED, BY OUR LOVE'S PROTECTION
I NO LONGER WALK AROUND BLUE

I'M SINCERELY SHAKING, AND THERE'S NO MISTAKING
YOUR LOVE IS MY FEVER WITHIN
THERE'S JUST NO DEBATING, IT'S JUST DEVASTATING
THAT WE SHARE A LOVE THAT WON'T END

I'M SAFE IN YOUR HAVEN, I STAY SO ELATED
FROM YOU LOVING ME TO THE BONE
NEVER UNDERRATED, NEVER SOMETHING FADED
NEVER WILL I NOW BE ALONE

I'M LOST OUT IN SPACE, YOUR BEAUTIFUL FACE
KEEPS ME FLOATING HIGH WITH THE STARS

YOU'RE MY MILKY WAY, WE'RE SO INTERLACED
YOU'RE RIGHT NEXT TO ME WHEN YOU'RE FAR

I'M NEVER THE SAME, I NOW WILL REMAIN
THIS MAN THAT YOU'VE TURNED INTO BOY
I'LL NEVER COMPLAIN, YOU'VE CAPTURED MY BRAIN
AND TURNED ALL MY PAIN INTO JOY

I'M ONLY THE HALF, OF YOUR AFTERMATH
FOR YOU HAVE TURNED ME INTO WHOLE
I'M NO LONELY MAN, SINCE WE HAVE BEGAN
SINCE THAT DAY MY HEART LOST CONTROL

I NO LONGER HIDE, I'VE STEPPED FROM BEHIND
THE WALL IN WHICH I USED TO LIVE
I NO LONGER FIND, ALL EMPTY IN MIND
YOUR LOVE HAS NOW GIVEN ME FILL

NO MEDICINE FOUND, NO POTION AROUND
COULD TAKE AWAY LOVE THAT'S SO PURE
NO SYRUP OR PILL, CAN DESTROY WHAT'S REAL
FOR THE LOVE WE SHARE THERE'S NO CURE

Out of Ink...

ONE DAY I SAT AND READ A BOOK OF TRUTH WRITTEN BY AN UNTRUSTWORTHY AUTHOR... DAZZLING WORDS AND PLOTS, ALL TO INTRIGUE THE UNSUSPECTING READER.
I GLANCED BACK AT HISTORY FOR ANSWERS TO SO MANY LINGERING QUESTIONS. THE KIND OF QUESTIONS THAT WE ARE ALL REQUIRED TO ASK OF OURSELVES, BUT NEVER DO!
DENIAL DOESN'T MAKE YOU BLIND...IT JUST MAKES YOU CLOSE YOUR EYES.
WHAT ARE THE QUESTIONS THAT WE PRESENT?
WHAT ARE THE ANSWERS WE SEEK?
WILL WE ONLY BE ABLE TO HEAR THE ANSWERS THAT LINE UP WITH HOW WE THINK?
AND HOW WOULD WE ANSWER THE QUESTIONS THAT HOLD US AND HAUNT US CONSTANTLY?

WHAT IS MY PURPOSE? WILL I HELP IT OR HURT IT?
WILL I BE WORTHY OR DESERVE IT?
HAVING EYES DOESN'T MEAN YOU CAN SEE...SIGHT WILL NEVER OUTWEIGH VISION.

DOES SOUND ONLY EXIST FOR THOSE WHO LISTEN?
DOES TOGETHER REALLY MEAN DIVISION?
SO MANY OF US HAVE EYES BUT OUR SIGHT IS MISSING!

PROGRAMMED TO WRITE OUR LIVES OUT ALL FOR WHAT THE READERS THINK
BUT THE READERS ONLY SEE US OUT OF INK…

Pages

OUR ENDLESS LOOK, AT OUR ENDLESS BOOK
THROUGH OUR EYES THAT SEE OUR STORY
OUR TIMELESS CLOCK, NOW OUR MINDS ARE LOCKED
ON ALL OUR LOVING GLORY
OUR BREATHLESS AIR, AND OUR STARE-LESS GLARE
INTO OUR AMAZING LINES
OUR SHIFTLESS MOVES, OUR RELUCTANT MOODS
THAT HELD OUR LOVE BEHIND
OUR TEARLESS SHEET, NOW OUR LIVES COMPLETE
BUT ONCE THERE WERE ONLY PIECES
OUR TREASURE FOUND, NOW WE BOTH ARE BOUND
TO EACH OTHER BY OUR DEEPNESS
OUR MISTY EYES, FROM OUR MISTY CRIES
FROM EMOTIONS FELT WITHIN
OUR DEEPEST SIGHS, FROM OUR STEEPEST HIGHS
FORE OUR LOVE NOW KNOWS NO END

OUR GENTLE KISS, FROM THE MENTAL BLISS
THAT WE SHARE EACH TIME WE TOUCH
OUR SIMPLE WISH, THAT ONE DAY THIS GIFT
WOULD FIND ITS WAY TO US
OUR LONELY NIGHTS, FROM OUR BLINDED SIGHTS
THAT WOULD PLAGUE US ONCE BEFORE
OUR ONLY FIGHT, WAS TO FIND THE LIGHT
THAT NOW GLOWS INSIDE OUR CORE
OUR STORY SHINES, IN A BOOK THAT BINDS
OUR LOVE FROM START TO FINISH
OUR MOUNTAIN CLIMBS, THROUGH THE HARDEST TIMES
AND OUR LOVE DID NOT DIMINISH
OUR COLDEST DAYS, AND OUR OLDEST WAYS
WHEN WE DWELLED WITHIN THE PAST
THE MOLD DID FADE, WE WERE SHOWN THE WAY
NOW OUR LOVE WILL FOREVER LAST
OUR LONELY FACE, FROM OUR LONELY SPACE
WHEN WE FLOATED THROUGH THE PAIN
OUR SUNNY DAY, PUSHED THE MUD AWAY
NOW WE FLOAT RIGHT THROUGH THE RAIN
OUR LONGEST FIGHT, TOOK OUR STRONGEST MIGHT
THOUGH IT SEEMED IT LASTED AGES
WE WROTE THE LINES, AND OUR LOVE SURVIVED
ALL OUR LOVE'S SUSPENSEFUL PAGES

Panic

THE SIRENS ROAR, THE MASSES SCATTER
BUT I STAND TALL AND STRONG
IT'S YOU THAT I HOLD, AND ALL THAT MATTERS
IS YOU WRAPPED IN MY ARMS
THE SCREAMERS YELL, THE TALKERS CHATTER
ALL SCRAMBLING LOST IN FEAR
THE DREAMERS FELL, ALL PAINTINGS SPLATTERED
I'M CALM WHEN YOU ARE HERE
THE STARS EXPLODE, BUT ALL ARE FLEEING
AND I JUST WATCH THEM FLEE
MY HEART AND SOUL, YOU ARE COMPLETING
YOUR LOVE CONSTRUCTED ME
THE TIME IS NOW, ALL CLOCKS HAVE VANISHED
DUE TO THE LOVE OF US
MY LIFE HAS FOUND, MY LIFE LONG HABIT
I'M LIVING FOR YOUR LOVE
THE WILD IS TAME, THE THUNDER'S SETTLED
MY SPIRIT FLOATS INSIDE
GOODBYE TO RAIN, IT'S SUN FOREVER
SINCE YOU BECAME MY BRIDE
THE FLIGHT HAS LANDED, OUR LOVE IS PLENTY

***ALL DEEPER THAN ROMANTIC
I COULD NOT MANAGE, COURAGE DIMINISHED
WITHOUT YOU, I WOULD PANIC***

Safety

MY MIND GOES BACK TO YESTERYEAR
WHEN MY HEARTBEAT WAS LOST
THE TIME I LACKED A SIGHT SO CLEAR
STILL BLINDED BY THE FROST
WITH COLD FILLED NIGHTS AND WINTER DAYS
I SHIVERED DAY AND EVE
NOW HOLDING TIGHT YOUR WARM EMBRACE
MY SHIVERING HAS CEASED
MY MIND RETURNS TO WINTER WINDS
COLLAPSING ALL MY HEART
AND NOW I'VE EARNED A LIFE-LONG FRIEND
OUR LOVE WILL NEVER PART
NO LONGER BOUND BY LONELINESS
FOR WE'VE BOTH BECOME ONE
NO LONGER FROWNS BUT JOY AND BLISS
YOU ARE MY SHINING SUN
I THINK BACK ON MY HARDEST TIMES
BEFORE WE INTERTWINED
MY MENTAL CRACKS MY DARKEST MINDS
INSIDE MY EMPTY SHRINE
I'VE BEEN RENEWED BECAUSE OF YOU

THE MUSIC NEVER STOPS
I'VE BEEN CONSUMED BY YOUR LOVE'S TUNE
ASCENSION NEVER DROPS
THE FEAR IS GONE I FEAR NO MORE
SINCE YOU HAVE EASED MY PAIN
MY DEAR, YOU'RE ALL THAT I ADORE
SINCE YOUR DEEP LOVE I'VE GAINED
YOU TOOK ME UP WHEN I WAS LOW
YOUR LOVE PROVIDED WINGS
YOU FILLED MY CUP AND MADE ME GLOW
AWAKENING MY DREAMS
A FANTASY IS WHAT YOU ARE
YOUR ABSENCE WOULD BREAK ME
THE DANGER IS GONE INSIDE MY HEART
YOUR LOVE'S MY HEART'S SAFETY

Severe

I'VE SEARCHED ALL MY LIFE TO NEVER FIND YOU
A TREASURE BEYOND THE UNFOUND
I'VE HEARD ALL THE LINES THAT NEVER RANG TRUE
THAT KEPT ME IN CIRCLES AROUND
I'VE READ ALL THE BOOKS DESIGNED FOR OUR BRAIN
TO PROMOTE THAT LOVE WOULD SURVIVE
I'VE SEEN ALL THE LOOKS FROM THOSE WHO BRING PAIN
AND LET US KNOW LOVE'S NOT ALIVE
I'VE FELT ALL THE AIR FROM FEELINGS NOT THERE
BUT YOU'VE MADE ME FEEL SUCH A GLOW
I FEEL ALL YOUR CARE ALL THE LOVE YOU SHARE
YOU CAME TO ME WRAPPED IN A BOW
I FEEL YOU'RE MY GIFT MY TRUE GRANTED WISH
YOU'RE MY REAL LIFE DREAM WHILE AWAKE
I NEED YOUR LOVE'S LIFT

YOUR LOVE IS EQUIPPED
TO ELEVATE ME ALL THE WAY
I BREATHE ALL YOUR BREATH
I STEP ALL YOUR STEPS
I WALK AS IF THERE IS NO PATH
I'M LOST IN YOUR SOUL UNTIL WE GROW OLD
'TIL DEATH IT'S YOUR LOVE THAT I HAVE
I DANCE FROM YOUR SONG YOU RIGHT ALL THAT'S WRONG
YOU'VE GIVEN ME POWER BEYOND
YOU'VE REMOVED ALL DOUBT OF WHAT LOVES ABOUT
TOGETHER FOR LIFE WE BELONG
I SEE ALL YOUR SIGHT, I NEED ALL YOUR LIGHT
THAT SHINES WHEN MY DARKNESS APPEARS
THE DEPTH DEEP INSIDE YOUR HEART AND YOUR MIND
IS PROOF THAT YOUR LOVE IS SEVERE

She

SHE LIVES INSIDE MY HEART AND MIND
RESIDING IN MY SOUL
AND GIVES MY STRIDE A FLOATING GLIDE
WHEN I WALK DOWN THE ROAD
SHE GIVES A SIGH INSIDE MY ARMS WHENEVER
I HOLD HER
AND GIVES MY EYE ITS GREATEST SPARK, LIKE
FIRE WHEN IT BURNS
SHE CARRIES ME WHEN I AM DOWN AND
SOOTHES ME THROUGH THE PAIN
AND BURYS GRIEF INTO THE GROUND
CONVERTING LOSS TO GAIN
SHE PUSHES ME WHEN I HAVE SLOWED
ENSURING I GO ON
AND LOOKS AT ME WITH EYES OF GOLD
I'VE NEEDED HER SO LONG
SHE WATCHES ME TO KNOW I'M SAFE
AND NEVER BATS AN EYE
AND OFTEN THINGS CAN TURN AND CHANGE
BUT NOT IN OUR LIFETIME
SHE STARTLES ME SO BEAUTIFULLY
EACH TIME I SEE HER FACE

AND ALL I SEE ENTRANCING ME
THROUGH ALL HER LOVE AND GRACE
SHE CALMS MY STORMS AND STOPS MY WARS
THE BATTLE IS NO MORE
WITH ALL MY CORE FOREVER MORE
IT'S HER I WILL ADORE
HER SULTRY WAYS AND LOVELY GAZE
JUST STOPS ME IN MY TRACKS
WITHOUT MY SANE I WILL REMAIN
LOST DEEP IN THIS ROMANCE
HER SIMPLE DAY IS LOVING ME
BEYOND A MEASURED DEPTH
WITH BLISSFUL DAZE HER LOVING WAYS
ADVANCING ALL MY STEPS
HER MYSTERY DWARFS MISERY AND HAPPINESS
ABIDES
WITH HISTORY OF HER AND ME
CONFIRMING WHAT'S INSIDE
I'LL NEVER KNOW HOW I COULD GO SO LONG
WITHOUT HER TOUCH
YOU'LL NEVER KNOW HOW I COULD GLOW
HOW I LOVE HER SO MUCH
I'LL NEVER HAVE ANOTHER CHANCE AT LOVE'S
ENCHANTED MADNESS
YOU'LL NEVER GLANCE AT ANOTHER MAN
SO FAR AWAY FROM SADNESS
I NEVER KNEW I'D FIND THE TRUTH AND SHE
WOULD CAPTURE ME
I'VE SEVERED GLOOM I'M NEVER BLUE DUE TO
THE LOVE OF SHE

Shiny

AND AWAY WE NOW GO OFF INTO THE SKY
THE MOMENT OUR HEARTS FEEL A BEAT
SOON AFTER WE KNOW BUT TO OUR DEMISE
THAT SWEETNESS IS NOT ALWAYS SWEET
OUR EYES OPEN WIDE BUT REALLY THEY SHUT
THE MOMENT EXCITEMENT INVADES
A PASSIONATE SIGH GIVES US SUCH A THRUST
INTO WHAT WILL SOON BRING OUR PAIN
IMMEDIATE LIFT FROM SIMPLY ONE KISS
THEN SUDDENLY FEELING DESIRE
A HOPE AND A WISH THAT LOVE WILL EXIST
THAT SUDDENLY THE FLAME WON'T EXPIRE
AND AWAY WE NOW GO OFF INTO THE BLISS
BELIEVING WE'VE FOUND WHAT IS REAL
A MASK AND A SHOW IS ALL THAT EXISTS
THAT ONLY IN TIME IS REVEALED
THAT COMFORTING TOUCH THAT SOOTHES US SO MUCH
WHILE LOST JUST ONE TOUCH SEEMS SINCERE
BUT SOON EVERY TOUCH CAN'T SOOTHE US ENOUGH
ONCE LIFE REVEALS ALL THAT WE FEARED

THAT ALL OF OUR HYPE THAT GAVE US OUR
FLIGHT
THAT MADE US SO BIG IS NOW TINY
THE PAIN NOW HAS MIGHT WE THOUGHT IT WAS
LIGHT
AGAIN WE WERE FOOLED BY THE SHINY

Stone

OUR LOVE IS BUT A ROCK, OUR BOULDER NEVER STOPS
OUR UNION IS A PILLAR OF PURE STRENGTH
OUR TRUST IS DEEP WITHIN, I TRUST I HAVE A FRIEND
FOR ALL OF LIFE WITHOUT A MEASURED LENGTH

OUR CREEK WILL EVER FLOW, HOW DEEP CAN WATERS GO
BEYOND A RIVER THAT WHICH WE COULD SWIM
OUR SIGHT IS NOT ENOUGH, TO SEE THE DEPTH OF US
BEYOND A VISION WHERE ALL SIGHT BEGINS

OUR VALLEY WILL EMBRACE, THE BEAUTY OF YOUR FACE
THE SIMPLE SIGHT OF YOU RENDERS ME STILL
OUR ROADS ARE PAVED IN GOLD, UNTIL WE BOTH GROW OLD
FOR YOU I WILL FOREVER CLIMB THE HILL

OUR SMOKE WILL HOVER HIGH, OUR FLAMES WILL ALWAYS RISE
THE PASSION WILL IGNITE FOREVER FLAMES
OUR SLOPE IS SOLID NOW, WE WILL NOW NEVER DOUBT
AND FOR ETERNITY OUR LOVE REMAINS

OUR PATH IS CRYSTAL CLEAR, OUR PATH NOW HOLDS NO FEAR
WE'VE OVERCOME THE ROCKY ROADS OF PAST
ROMANCE IS IN OUR HEARTS, NO CHANCE THAT WE WILL PART
FOR NOW WE SHARE THE DEEPEST LOVE AT LAST

OUR WHISPER IS NOW LOUD, OUR HISTORY PROFOUND
NO MORE WILL WE SLEEP LONELY IN OUR DREAMS
OUR VICTORY IS FOUND, OUR LOVE IS NOW THE SOUND
THAT MELODY THAT NOW FOREVER SINGS

OUR HEARTS ARE NOW THE BEAT, THAT MAKE OUR LIVES COMPLETE
WE LOVE EACH OTHER WELL BEYOND THE WORD
OUR SPARK IS BRIGHTLY SEEN, WE NOW FOREVER LEAN
ON BOTH OUR HEARTS HIGH SOARING LIKE A BIRD

OUR UNION IS NOW ONE, WE'VE ONLY JUST BEGUN
NO MORE WE WILL BE LIVING LIFE ALONE
OUR ROCK HAS FINALLY FORMED, NOW OUR LOVE HAS CONFORMED
US BOTH INTO ONE LIFE WRITTEN IN STONE

Thorns

IT SEEMS TO START OFF AS A FLOWER
THE EYE SEES A BEAUTIFUL BLOOM
IT SEEMS THAT THE BULBS GIVE US POWER
BUT TRUE POWER COMES FROM THE GLOOM

IT SEEMS WE ALL SEARCH FOR THE DAISIES
BUT WE OVERLOOK ALL THE STEMS
IT SEEMS THAT WE LOSE FROM THE MAYBES
OUR LEAVES BLOW AWAY WITH THE WIND

IT SEEMS WE GET FOOLED BY THE LILIES
WE INVEST ALL TRUTH IN THEIR LIGHT
IT SEEMS WE DON'T LOOK AT THEM REALLY
WE ONLY LOOK FOR THE DELIGHT

IT SEEMS WE ONLY LOVE THE PEDALS
UNTIL WE REALIZE THEY'RE A PLANT
IT SEEMS THAT OUR MINDS NEVER SETTLE
WE NEED TO SEE TRUTH BUT WE CAN'T

IT SEEMS THAT THE SOIL IS THE FINEST
UNTIL WE PLANT ALL OF THE SEEDS

IT SEEMS WHAT WAS PLUS IS A MINUS
THINGS JUST AREN'T WHAT WE BELIEVED

IT SEEMS THAT THE TREE HAD FRESH APPLES
BUT WE COULDN'T SEE PAST THE LEAVES
IT SEEMS THAT WHEN IN LIFE WE GRAPPLE
IT LIFTS US TO OVERCOME THINGS

IT SEEMED THAT THE BUSH WAS STILL BLOOMING
UNTIL WE COULD SEE THAT IT STOPPED
IT SEEMED WE WOULD WIN BUT WE'RE LOSING
WHAT ONCE SEEMED SO HIGH HAS NOW DROPPED

IT SEEMED THAT WE FOUND THE TRUE POTION
WE FINALLY SAW PAST ALL THE STORMS
BUT WE CAN'T ENJOY ALL THE ROSES
UNLESS WE SURVIVE ALL THE THORNS

Tick Tock

I LOOK FOR A WAY TO SETTLE DOWN
UNTIL YOU'RE IN MY ARMS AGAIN
I SUFFER THE MOMENT YOU'RE NOT AROUND
AND TIME SEEMS TO STAND STILL AND END
I LOOK FOR THE NIGHTS I'M HOLDING YOU
AND YOU'RE LAYING RIGHT BY MY SIDE
YOUR PRESENCE PROVIDES MY ONLY SOOTHE
AND IN YOUR TOUCH I STILL CONFIDE
I LOOK FOR YOUR FACE YOUR TENDER LIPS
THE SIGHT OF YOU MAKES ME A KING
I LOOK FOR THE TASTE OF YOUR GENTLE KISS
ONE KISS MOVES THE SOUL OF MY BEING
I LOOK FOR YOUR VOICE SO I CAN HEAR
THE MELODIES SUNG BY YOUR WORDS
THE MOMENT YOU SPOKE INTO MY EAR
SOFT MUSIC WAS ALL THAT I HEARD
I LOOK FOR THE SCENT OF YOUR PERFUME
IT LINGERS EACH TIME THAT YOU LEAVE
MY SMELLING EXISTS BECAUSE OF YOU
MY NOSE STILL INHALES FOR YOUR BREEZE
I LOOK FOR YOUR HANDS TO COMFORT ME
WHENEVER I FEEL DOWN AND OUT

YOUR LOVE STILL PROVIDES MY COMFORTING
NO COMFORT WHEN YOU'RE NOT AROUND
I LOOK FOR YOUR LAUGH WHEN THERE'S A JOKE
YOUR GIGGLING WAYS BRING ME PEACE
I DON'T STAND A CHANCE I'M WITHOUT HOPE
IF YOUR TENDER LOVE WERE TO CEASE
I LOOK FOR A WAY TO FILL THE TIME
WHEN YOU LEAVE, ALL TIME SEEMS TO STOP
UNTIL YOUR RETURN I'M STANDING BY
JUST WATCHING THE CLOCK GO TICK TOCK

Trauma

I THINK OF THE TIME BEFORE I MET YOU
MY MIND WAS SO ENDLESSLY BLUE
I THINK BACK ON WHEN WE WERE JUST TWO
JUST WANDERING BY WITH NO CLUE
I THINK OF MY MIND BEFORE IT WAS FILLED
WITH HOW MUCH YOU BRING ME A THRILL
I THINK OF THE LIE BEFORE THE REAL
OUR HEARTS WERE SO COLD THEY WERE CHILLED
I THINK OF THE SOUND OF LONELY NIGHTS
WHEN WE WERE WITHOUT OUR LOVE LIFE
BUT NOW YOU ARE MINE TO OUR DELIGHT
NO LONGER ARE WE WITHOUT SIGHT
I THINK OF A WISH INSIDE OUR HEADS
BELIEVING THAT ALL LOVE WAS DEAD
BUT NOW WE'VE FOUND LOVE FORE WE WERE LEAD
TO EACH OTHER'S EMBRACE INSTEAD
I THINK OF THE HOPE I JUST FORGOT
BECAUSE OF HOW LOVE WAS JUST NOT
AND HOW ALL RELATIONS WOULD SIMPLY FLOP

NOW YOUR LOVE TOOK ME TO THE TOP
I THINK OF THE SMILES I LIVED WITHOUT
WHEN MY MIND WAS FULL OF JUST DOUBT
I THINK OF THE CRIES I SHOUTED OUT
SHOUTING FOR WHAT NOW I HAVE FOUND
I THINK OF THE NIGHTS WHEN I WOULD HOLLER
CONSUMED BY MY LONELY LIFES DRAMA
BUT NOW YOU ARE MINE YOU ARE MY KARMA
YOUR ABSENCE WOULD CAUSE MY HEART TRAUMA

Unconscious

WE'RE BORN INTO LIFE BEGINNING OUR STRIFE
THEN SUDDENLY WE'RE FED MEALS OF THOUGHT
INFORMED ALL OUR LIFE WHAT'S WRONG AND WHAT'S RIGHT
BELIEVING WE'RE FOUND BUT WE'RE LOST
INJECTED WITH LIES CONSUMING OUR MINDS
CONTROLLING THE SCENES AS WE ACT
INFECTED WITH KNIVES SOON WHAT ONCE SEEMED WISE
IS SUDDENLY DEMOLISHED BY FACT
OUR PASSION IGNITES THE LIES WE INVITE
AS FEEDERS KEEP FILLING OUR PLATES
OUR PASSIONATE VIBE MAKES US FEEL ALIVE
WHILE LOCKING OURSELVES INSIDE GATES
OUR EYES ONLY SEE WHAT WE CHOOSE TO BELIEVE
FORE SEEING THE TRUTH MAKES US BLIND
OUR LIVES ONLY MEAN WHAT WE CAN CONCEIVE
ENTRAPPED IN THE JAIL OF OUR MIND

ENSLAVED IN OUR SOULS TILL WE ALL GROW OLD
WHILE LIVING OUR LIVES BY THE RULES
ENGAGED IN OUR HOMES THE MORE THAT WE KNOW
MAKES WISE MEN REALIZE THEY'VE BEEN FOOLS
WE WALK WITHOUT LEGS WE THINK WITHOUT HEADS
CONVICTED TO SERVE ALL THE AUTHORS
WHO WROTE ALL THE LINES CONTROLLING OUR MINDS
WHILE MAKING US SICK FOR THE DOCTORS
THE CIRCLE COMES BACK STARTING A NEW ACT
DECEPTION FLIES HIGHER THEN ROCKETS
A NEW LIFE IN TACT DESIGNED TO ATTRACT
THE SOULS OF ALL WHO ARE UNCONSCIOUS

WE

WE ARE A FIGMENT OF MY MIND
WHAT WE HAVE IS SO REAL I MUST FIND WAYS
TO SEE ITS TRUTH
WE ARE THE COUNTER OF ALL LIES
WHAT PEOPLE CLAIM THEY FEEL IS DEFINED
BY WHAT THEY DO
WE HAVE CONQUERED ALL MYTHS
WHAT WE HAVE IS SO DEEP THAT TO OTHERS IT
WILL NOT REFLECT
WE HAVE UNWRAPPED A GIFT
BUT THE OTHERS WON'T SEE ITS TRUE
STRENGTH AND TRUE DEPTH
WE HAVE BEEN SHOWN THE LIGHT
AND DELIVERED FROM DARKNESS IN WHICH
OTHERS STILL RELY
WE KNOW LOVE'S PATH IS BRIGHT
FEELING IT'S SPARK AND JUST KNOWING FOR
LIFE YOU'LL BE RIGHT BY MY SIDE
WE LOOK TOWARDS THE FUTURE
AND THE BLISS THAT WE SHARE FROM THE
LOVE THAT WE BARE RENDERS US USELESS
WE BOTH NEED A SUTURE

THE HEARTS THAT WOULD BREAK IF WE JUST WALKED AWAY WOULD LEAVE PERMANENT BRUISES
WE LOVE ON A LEVEL
THAT OTHERS COULD NEVER RELATE TO ANY PART OF OUR UNION
WE CAN REMOVE THE SHOVEL
THAT WON'T STOP THE CRITICS FROM CONSTANTLY DIGGING TO CAUSE US CONFUSION
WE JUST CAN'T MAKE SENSE
OF THE WAYS THEY ALL PREY ON THE JOY OF LOVE'S MAGIC
WE CAN'T JUST DISMISS
THAT THE HATERS AND NON-RELATERS HAVE ONLY WITNESSED LOVE TRAGIC
WE HAVE ALL WE NEED
IN EACH OTHER WE CAN HOVER ON OUR OWN CLOUD OF US
WE CAN ONLY BE WEAK
IF WE ALLOW OTHERS TO CAUSE US DISRUPTION AND DESTROY OUR TRUST

WE ARE DEEPER THAN THAT...
WHY CAN'T THEY ALL SEE?
THERE'S NOT A DEEPER TWO IN LOVE THAN WE...

Winter

I CAN FEEL THE CHILLS FROM THE OUTER WIND
AND STILL THIS IS MY FAVORITE SEASON
NOW IT FEELS UNREAL ALL THE LOVE THAT I FEEL
AND MY DEAR YOU'RE THE ONE SINGLE REASON
I CAN NOT UNDERSTAND HOW YOUR PRESENCE COMMANDS
ALL ATTENTION FROM ME EVERY SECOND
YOU UPLIFT ME MY LOVE AND MY GIFT IS YOUR HUG
YOUR EMBRACE CONVEYS ALL YOUR AFFECTION
I CAN LOVE YOU FOREVER YOUR TOUCH SOFT AS A FEATHER
AND THE TENDER WITHIN IS UNMATCHED
YOU'RE THE GENTLE IN ME JUST THE GENTLE I NEED
IN THIS WORLD FULL OF THORNS I'M UNSCRATCHED
YOU'RE MY HEARTBEAT OF HOPE YOU'RE THE REASON I COPE
WITH THIS UNYIELDING WORLD OF DISMAY
YOU INSPIRE MY WILL AND DEMOLISH MY HILLS
I WILL NO LONGER LIVE LIFE IN PAIN

I CAN SEE YOUR SMILE AND YOU'RE JUST LIKE A CHILD
YOU MAKE MY DEEP HEART WANT TO PLAY
AND I'M DANCING AROUND AS I HEAR THUNDER SOUND
YOU MAKE ME LOOK FORWARD TO RAIN
WE'LL BE CUDDLING CLOSE LOCKED IN EACH OTHER'S HOLD
AS WE LISTEN TO RAIN HIT THE ROOF
OUR EYES LOCKED IN A GAZE OUR TRUE LOVE IT'S AMAZE
MAKES A THUNDEROUS STORM ALL SEEM MUTE
I CAN FEEL YOUR PULSE IT'S THE LOVE OF US
THAT KEEP US BOTH WARM WHEN IT'S SNOWING
I CAN READ YOUR MIND ALL YOUR THOUGHTS INSIDE
ARE AS MINE AND THAT'S WHY WE'RE BOTH GLOWING
NOW IT'S COLD OUTDOORS BUT I TWITCH NO MORE
SINCE THE DAY YOU BECAME ALL MY HEAT
YOU'RE MY FIREPLACE ON THE COLDEST DAY
YOUR LOVE IS THE FLAME THAT WARMS ME
I CAN HEAR YOUR MOANS AND YOUR SIGHS OF PASSION
AND THE COLD AND THE RAIN DO NOT ENTER
BUT THE WARMTH YOU SHOW WHEN THE WEATHER'S CRASHING
IS THE REASON I SO LOVE THE WINTER

Youphoric

I STILL UNBELIEVE THE SOUND OF YOUR
VOICE
THE MOMENT YOU UTTER A WORD
I STILL INCONCEIVE THAT I AM YOUR CHOICE
THE CRIES OF MY LOVE WERE UNHEARD
I STILL UNBELIEVE THE GLOW OF YOUR
SMILE
EACH TIME I SEE JOY IN YOUR FACE
I STILL INCONCEIVE THE FLOW OF YOUR
MILD
I'M NOW IN AN UNCONSCIOUS PLACE
I STILL UNBELIEVE THE SHINE OF YOUR
GLOW
EACH TIME I SEE YOUR LIGHT APPEAR
I STILL INCONCEIVE THE WARMTH OF YOUR
HOLD
EACH TIME YOU ARE HOLDING ME NEAR
I STILL UNBELIEVE THE PIERCE OF YOUR
GLARE
EACH TIME THAT I LOOK IN YOUR EYES
I STILL INCONCEIVE THE FIERCE OF YOUR
STARE

ONE LOOK RENDERS ME HYPNOTIZED
I STILL UNBELIEVE THE CLOSENESS I FEEL
EVEN WHEN YOU'RE SO FAR AWAY
I STILL INCONCEIVE THIS WOKENESS IS REAL
YOU MAKE ME FEEL SLEEP EVERYDAY
I STILL UNBELIEVE THAT POWER OF YOU
YOUR LIGHTING IGNITING MY HEART
I STILL INCONCEIVE THE HOUR OF TRUTH
REVEALING THAT WE WILL NOT PART
I STILL UNBELIEVE THIS VISION OF MINE
SEEING YOU RUN INTO MY ARMS
I STILL INCONCEIVE ENVISIONING TIME
COMPLETELY ENTRAPPED BY YOUR CHARM
I STILL UNBELIEVE ILLUSIONS OF LOVE
KNOWING THAT I CAN NOT IGNORE IT
I STILL INCONCEIVE THIS VISION OF US
MY STATE WILL NOW REMAIN YOUPHORIC